Made in the USA
Monee, IL
07 October 2022

15408030R00070